EMMANUEL JOSEPH

Invisible Wings: Soaring to New Heights Within

Copyright © 2025 by Emmanuel Joseph

All rights reserved. No part of this publication may be reproduced, stored or transmitted in any form or by any means, electronic, mechanical, photocopying, recording, scanning, or otherwise without written permission from the publisher. It is illegal to copy this book, post it to a website, or distribute it by any other means without permission.

First edition

*This book was professionally typeset on Reedsy.
Find out more at reedsy.com*

Contents

1	Chapter 1: The Seed of Transformation	1
2	Chapter 2: Whispering Winds	3
3	Chapter 3: Embracing the Unknown	5
4	Chapter 4: The Power of Connection	7
5	Chapter 5: Facing the Shadows	8
6	Chapter 6: The Echoes of Ancestors	9
7	Chapter 7: The Dance of Dreams	10
8	Chapter 8: The Alchemy of Love	11
9	Chapter 9: The Summit of Self	12
10	Chapter 10: Ripples of Change	13
11	Chapter 11: Embracing the Future	14
12	Chapter 12: The Legacy of Invisible Wings	15

1

Chapter 1: The Seed of Transformation

In the quiet town of Nuru, where every morning the sun cast a golden hue over the bustling market, lived a young girl named Adanna. To everyone around, she was simply another face in the crowd, but within her resided an unfulfilled yearning, a dream that seemed too grand for her modest world. She often found herself staring at the sky, imagining what it would be like to soar like the eagles, to see the world from above and feel the freedom in her veins.

Adanna's family was close-knit, their lives intertwined with the rhythms of the village. Her parents, hardworking farmers, had always taught her the value of dedication and perseverance. Yet, despite her love for them, Adanna felt a disconnect, a sense of belonging to something larger than the fields and the narrow paths of Nuru. She felt an invisible set of wings aching to spread, yet bound by the gravity of her reality.

One day, while wandering through the outskirts of the village, Adanna stumbled upon an old library, forgotten by time and the hustle of daily life. The moment she stepped inside, she felt an inexplicable connection, as if the walls whispered secrets of ancient wisdom and untold stories. The air was thick with the scent of old books, and Adanna felt her heart race with excitement and a strange sense of destiny.

Among the dusty shelves, she found a book with a cover that shimmered faintly in the dim light. It was titled "The Alchemy of the Soul," and as she opened its pages, she was greeted by stories of legendary figures who had transcended their earthly bounds, achieving greatness through self-discovery and inner strength. This book became her silent mentor, guiding her through the first steps of a journey that would transform her life forever.

2

Chapter 2: Whispering Winds

As the days turned into weeks, Adanna found herself engrossed in the tales and teachings within "The Alchemy of the Soul." Each chapter seemed to unlock a new facet of her spirit, revealing the potential that lay dormant within her. She learned about the power of intention, the art of mindfulness, and the importance of nurturing one's inner world to manifest external realities. The more she read, the more she felt her invisible wings unfurling.

One evening, while sitting by the river that flowed through Nuru, Adanna noticed a peculiar sight. An elderly woman, cloaked in a vibrant shawl, was sitting on a rock, seemingly meditating. Her presence exuded a sense of calm and wisdom that drew Adanna closer. Intrigued, she approached the woman, who opened her eyes and greeted Adanna with a warm smile.

The woman introduced herself as Nkem, a healer and a guide who had traveled the world, learning the ancient arts of inner transformation and spiritual growth. Sensing Adanna's curiosity and potential, Nkem decided to mentor her, to help her cultivate her newfound abilities and soar to the heights she dreamed of. This encounter marked the beginning of a profound friendship and a transformative journey that would shape Adanna's future.

Under Nkem's guidance, Adanna learned to harness the energy within her, to meditate and connect with the elements around her. They spent hours by the river, practicing breathing exercises and visualizations, allowing

Adanna to tap into her inner strength and intuition. Nkem taught her about the interconnectedness of all life, the delicate balance between giving and receiving, and the importance of living in harmony with nature.

As Adanna progressed, she began to notice subtle changes within herself. Her senses became sharper, her mind clearer, and her heart lighter. She felt a newfound sense of purpose and confidence, a deep knowing that she was on the right path. With each passing day, her invisible wings grew stronger, ready to lift her to new heights.

3

Chapter 3: Embracing the Unknown

Emboldened by her growing abilities and Nkem's teachings, Adanna began to explore the world beyond Nuru. She ventured into neighboring villages, seeking out new experiences and opportunities to learn from others. Her journey was not without challenges, but each obstacle she faced only served to strengthen her resolve and deepen her understanding of herself and the world around her.

In one village, she met a group of artisans who created beautiful works of art from natural materials. Adanna was captivated by their craftsmanship and dedication, and she spent several weeks learning their techniques and discovering the joy of creating something with her own hands. The experience taught her the importance of patience, persistence, and the beauty that can be found in even the simplest of things.

During her travels, Adanna also encountered individuals who had overcome great adversity to achieve their dreams. Their stories of resilience and determination inspired her to continue pushing forward, no matter how difficult the journey might be. She realized that her invisible wings were not just a symbol of her potential, but a testament to the strength and courage that resided within her.

As she embraced the unknown and ventured further from home, Adanna discovered a sense of freedom and exhilaration she had never known before. She felt as if the world was opening up to her, revealing its mysteries and wonders one by one. With each new experience, she grew more confident in her ability to navigate the challenges of life and to soar to heights she had once only dreamed of.

4

Chapter 4: The Power of Connection

Through her travels, Adanna discovered the profound impact of human connection. She met people from all walks of life, each with their own unique stories, struggles, and triumphs. These encounters enriched her understanding of the world and deepened her empathy for others.

In one bustling city, Adanna joined a community of volunteers who dedicated their time to helping those in need. She worked alongside them, offering her skills and support to uplift the lives of others. Through this experience, she learned the importance of compassion, generosity, and the transformative power of kindness.

Adanna also found herself forming deep bonds with those she met along the way. She cherished the moments of laughter, shared wisdom, and mutual support that came from these connections. These relationships became a source of strength and inspiration, reminding her of the interconnectedness of all beings and the power of unity.

As Adanna continued to grow and evolve, she realized that her journey was not just about personal transformation, but about contributing to the greater good. She felt a calling to use her newfound abilities and insights to make a positive impact on the world around her. With her invisible wings fully unfurled, she was ready to soar to new heights and embrace her destiny.

5

Chapter 5: Facing the Shadows

Despite her newfound strength and clarity, Adanna soon realized that her journey was far from over. She began to encounter moments of doubt and fear that threatened to weigh her down. These internal struggles, often more daunting than any external challenge, required her to confront the shadows within herself.

With Nkem's guidance, Adanna learned to embrace these difficult emotions rather than avoid them. She practiced self-reflection and journaling, allowing herself to explore the depths of her fears and insecurities. Through this process, she discovered that her invisible wings were not just tools for soaring to new heights but also for navigating the valleys and shadows within her soul.

One night, while sitting by a fire under a starlit sky, Adanna shared her innermost thoughts and fears with Nkem. The wise healer listened patiently and then spoke of the importance of balance – the need to accept both light and shadow as essential parts of the human experience. Nkem reminded Adanna that true strength comes from acknowledging and integrating all aspects of oneself.

This profound insight helped Adanna find a sense of peace and resilience. She understood that her journey was not about eradicating fear but about cultivating the courage to face it. With this newfound perspective, she felt her wings grow stronger, ready to carry her through any storm.

6

Chapter 6: The Echoes of Ancestors

As Adanna continued her journey, she felt a deepening connection to her heritage and the wisdom of her ancestors. She visited sacred sites and spoke with elders who shared stories of their own journeys and the lessons they had learned along the way. These encounters enriched her understanding of her cultural roots and the collective strength of her people.

In one village, Adanna met an elder named Adebayo, who was renowned for his knowledge of the ancient traditions and spiritual practices of their ancestors. Adebayo taught Adanna about the importance of rituals and ceremonies in honoring the past and staying connected to one's lineage. Through these teachings, she discovered a sense of belonging and continuity that grounded her in her quest for self-discovery.

Adanna also learned about the concept of "Ubuntu," a philosophy that emphasizes the interconnectedness of all people and the idea that one's humanity is intrinsically tied to the humanity of others. This understanding deepened her sense of empathy and compassion, reinforcing the importance of community and collective growth.

Inspired by the wisdom of her ancestors, Adanna felt a renewed sense of purpose and commitment to her journey. She realized that her invisible wings were not just for her own flight but also for lifting others and contributing to the greater good.

7

Chapter 7: The Dance of Dreams

A danna's journey brought her to a vibrant city where she encountered a community of dreamers and visionaries. These individuals, each pursuing their unique passions and aspirations, inspired her to embrace her own dreams with renewed vigor. She immersed herself in their world, learning from their experiences and drawing strength from their collective energy.

In this city, Adanna met a young artist named Chike, whose paintings captured the beauty and complexity of the human spirit. Chike's work resonated deeply with Adanna, reminding her of the power of creativity and self-expression. The two quickly became friends, and Adanna found herself inspired to explore her own artistic talents.

Through her interactions with Chike and other artists, Adanna discovered the joy of creating and the freedom that came from expressing herself authentically. She realized that her invisible wings were not just for soaring to new heights but also for dancing through the tapestry of life, weaving her unique essence into the world.

With each new creation, Adanna felt a sense of fulfillment and connection to her inner self. She embraced the dance of dreams, understanding that her journey was not just about reaching a destination but about experiencing the beauty and wonder of the journey itself.

8

Chapter 8: The Alchemy of Love

As Adanna's journey continued, she found herself reflecting on the importance of love in its many forms. She had experienced the love of family, the support of friends, and the kindness of strangers. These connections had enriched her life and fueled her growth.

One day, while exploring a serene garden, Adanna encountered a young man named Eze. Their connection was instant and profound, as if they had known each other in a previous lifetime. Eze, a gentle and wise soul, shared Adanna's passion for self-discovery and inner growth. Their bond quickly deepened, and they became each other's confidants and partners in exploration.

Through their relationship, Adanna learned about the transformative power of love. Eze's unwavering support and understanding provided her with a sense of security and encouragement. Together, they faced challenges, celebrated victories, and grew in their individual and shared journeys.

Adanna realized that love was the ultimate alchemist, capable of turning the ordinary into the extraordinary. It was the force that connected her to the world and the people around her, lifting her to new heights and helping her navigate the depths. With Eze by her side, Adanna felt her invisible wings soar even higher, buoyed by the strength of their love.

9

Chapter 9: The Summit of Self

Adanna's journey led her to a secluded mountain, known to the villagers as the "Summit of Self." Legends spoke of the profound transformations experienced by those who dared to climb its rugged paths. With Eze by her side and Nkem's teachings in her heart, Adanna felt ready to take on this final challenge.

The ascent was grueling, testing both their physical and mental endurance. They faced treacherous terrain, harsh weather, and moments of doubt. But with each step, Adanna felt herself growing stronger, her invisible wings carrying her through the toughest trials. The climb was a metaphor for her internal journey, each challenge a reflection of the shadows she had faced and overcome.

At the peak, Adanna stood on the edge of the world, gazing out at the vast expanse before her. The view was breathtaking, a reminder of the boundless possibilities that lay ahead. In that moment of serenity and triumph, she felt a profound connection to herself, to Eze, to Nkem, and to all the people who had touched her life.

Adanna realized that the summit was not a destination, but a milestone in her ongoing journey of growth and self-discovery. She understood that her invisible wings would continue to evolve, carrying her to new heights and deeper understandings. With gratitude and determination, she embraced the limitless potential within her.

10

Chapter 10: Ripples of Change

As Adanna descended the mountain, she felt a renewed sense of purpose. She was determined to share the wisdom and insights she had gained with others, to inspire and uplift those who were still searching for their own invisible wings. Her journey had transformed her, and she was eager to make a positive impact on the world.

Back in Nuru, Adanna started a community center where people could come together to learn, grow, and support one another. She offered workshops on mindfulness, creative expression, and self-discovery, sharing the teachings that had guided her on her path. The center became a sanctuary for those seeking solace and inspiration, a place where dreams could take flight.

Adanna's efforts created ripples of change that spread throughout the village and beyond. People began to embrace their own journeys of transformation, discovering the power within themselves to overcome challenges and reach new heights. The community thrived, united by a shared commitment to growth and connection.

Adanna's invisible wings had not only lifted her but had also inspired others to find their own. The spirit of Nkem's teachings and the love of Eze continued to guide her, reminding her that the journey was as important as the destination. Together, they created a legacy of hope, resilience, and the belief that anyone could soar to new heights within.

11

Chapter 11: Embracing the Future

Years passed, and Adanna's community center became a beacon of hope and transformation for people from all walks of life. The impact of her work was evident in the countless lives that had been touched and transformed. Adanna continued to grow and evolve, always seeking new ways to inspire and uplift those around her.

Eze, now her lifelong partner, stood by her side through every triumph and challenge. Their love had deepened and matured, a testament to the power of connection and mutual support. Together, they faced the future with courage and optimism, knowing that their journey was far from over.

Adanna also maintained her bond with Nkem, who had become a revered elder in the community. Nkem's wisdom and guidance remained a cornerstone of Adanna's work, reminding her of the importance of humility, gratitude, and continuous growth. The lessons she had learned from Nkem continued to shape her journey, guiding her as she embraced the future.

With each new generation that came to the community center, Adanna saw the legacy of her journey unfold. She felt a profound sense of fulfillment, knowing that her invisible wings had not only lifted her but had also empowered others to soar. Her story was a testament to the transformative power of self-discovery, connection, and love.

12

Chapter 12: The Legacy of Invisible Wings

As the years went by, Adanna's story became a legend, passed down through generations as a source of inspiration and hope. The community center she had founded continued to thrive, a testament to the enduring impact of her journey. The teachings of "The Alchemy of the Soul," the wisdom of Nkem, and the love of Eze were woven into the fabric of the community, guiding and uplifting all who came to seek their own transformation.

Adanna's invisible wings had become a symbol of the limitless potential that resided within every individual. Her journey had shown that true strength came from within, and that the path to self-discovery was a lifelong quest. The legacy of her story inspired countless others to embark on their own journeys, to embrace the challenges and triumphs that awaited them.

In the quiet moments of reflection, Adanna felt a deep sense of gratitude for the life she had lived and the impact she had made. She knew that her journey was far from over, that there were still new heights to soar to and new horizons to explore. With her invisible wings unfurled, she faced the future with an open heart and a boundless spirit.

And so, the story of Adanna and her invisible wings continued, a testament to the power of transformation, the strength of the human spirit, and the infinite possibilities that lay within us all. Her legacy lived on in the hearts and minds of those who believed in the magic of their own journeys, soaring to new heights within and beyond.

Book Description

Invisible Wings: Soaring to New Heights Within

In the quiet village of Nuru, a young girl named Adanna feels a yearning to soar beyond her humble life. As she discovers an old book titled "The Alchemy of the Soul," she embarks on a transformative journey of self-discovery and inner growth. With the guidance of the wise healer Nkem and the support of her loving partner Eze, Adanna learns to embrace her potential and navigate the challenges of life.

Through encounters with diverse individuals, ancient traditions, and the power of human connection, Adanna's invisible wings unfurl, lifting her to new heights. Her journey becomes a testament to the strength of the human spirit, the importance of community, and the boundless possibilities that lie within us all.

Join Adanna as she faces her fears, embraces her dreams, and creates a legacy of hope and resilience in "Invisible Wings: Soaring to New Heights Within." This inspiring tale reminds us that true transformation comes from within and that we all have the power to soar to new heights.

www.ingramcontent.com/pod-product-compliance
Lightning Source LLC
LaVergne TN
LVHW020509080526
838202LV00057B/6269